BAFFLING BEHAVIOR IN THE PAST

ROAR!

LIFE IN ANCIENT ROME

by Noah Leatherland

BEARPORT
PUBLISHING

Minneapolis, Minnesota

Credits
Images are courtesy of Shutterstock.com. With thanks to Getty Images, Thinkstock Photo, Wikimedia Media Commons, and iStockphoto. COVER & RECURRING – JORDEN MARBLE, luckyraccoon, ONYXprj, PCH.Vector. 4–5 – Vlas Telino studio, Sidhe, Anna Iamanova. 6–7 – Kraft74, Morphart Creation, ONYXprj, Art UK. 8–9 – AlexAnton, Kuhn, Public domain, via Wikimedia Commons, Galina Sinelnikova, Ulpiano Checa. 10–11 – Matankic, CC BY-SA 4.0 <https://creativecommons.org/licenses/by-sa/4.0>, via Wikimedia Commons, ZenitX. 12–13 – BEAUTY STUDIO, autbmoore, Kovaleva_Ka, Dmitriy Kazitsyn, baldezh, Leestudio, chengyuzheng, Irina Nedikova. 14–15 – domnitsky, zevana, Nick N A, xpixel. 16–17 – LouieLea, Evannovostro. 18–19 – Koca Vehbi, fotopanorama360, Natalllenka.m, WinWin artlab. 20–21 – SergeyKlopotov, Yair Haklai, CC BY-SA 4.0 <https://creativecommons.org/licenses/by-sa/4.0>, via Wikimedia Commons. 22–23 – WH_Pics, Laurent Renault. 24–25 – isawnyu, CC BY 2.0 <https://creativecommons.org/licenses/by/2.0>, via Wikimedia Commons, Tomasz Guzowski. 26–27 – Geza Farkas, Carole Raddato from FRANKFURT, Germany, CC BY-SA 2.0 <https://creativecommons.org/licenses/by-sa/2.0>, via Wikimedia Commons. 28–29 – staff.4j.lane.edu, Public domain, via Wikimedia Commons, Eivaisla, Akarawut, Dora Zett, Billion Photos, PetlinDmitry, NotionPic. 30 – BlackMac.

Bearport Publishing Company Product Development Team
Publisher: Jen Jenson; Director of Product Development: Spencer Brinker; Managing Editor: Allison Juda; Editor: Cole Nelson; Associate Editor: Naomi Reich; Associate Editor: Tiana Tran; Art Director: Colin O'Dea; Designer: Kim Jones; Designer: Kayla Eggert; Product Development Specialist: Owen Hamlin

Library of Congress Cataloging-in-Publication Data is available at www.loc.gov or upon request from the publisher.

ISBN: 979-8-89232-882-1 (hardcover)
ISBN: 979-8-89232-968-2 (paperback)
ISBN: 979-8-89232-912-5 (ebook)

For more information, write to Bearport Publishing, 5357 Penn Avenue South, Minneapolis, MN 55419.

CONTENTS

ANCIENT ROME

Life in ancient Rome was full of rich history . . . and baffling behavior! Looking back, some of the stories we hear from ancient Rome may seem strange.

The city of Rome was founded in 753 BCE. The **civilization** that started with this city lasted for more than 1,000 years.

BCE MEANS BEFORE THE COMMON ERA. THIS IS THE TIME BEFORE THE YEAR 0.

Ancient Rome started as a small town that eventually grew much larger. First, ancient Rome was ruled by kings. Then, it was managed as a **republic**. Ancient Rome later became an empire ruled by emperors.

ASIA

EUROPE

Atlantic Ocean

Mediterranean Sea

AFRICA

N
W   E
S

☐ **THE ROMAN EMPIRE**

At its biggest, the Roman Empire spread across parts of Europe, Asia, and Africa. There were around 100 million people living in the empire.

THE EMPIRE'S EMPERORS

Emperors were the most important people in ancient Rome. There were some things that only the emperors were allowed to do.

In ancient Rome, the emperor was the only person who could wear the color purple. If anyone else dressed in the color, they would be punished. Some people were even killed for it.

EMPEROR NERO

Emperor Nero loved to sing, whether people liked it or not. When he performed, Emperor Nero had 5,000 soldiers clap for him.

EMPEROR CALIGULA

Emperors often got away with their strange behavior. That's how powerful they were! Emperor Caligula wanted everyone to treat him like a god. He even tried to make his horse a **politician**.

THE COLOSSEUM

Emperor Vespasian thought that Roman people needed entertainment. So, he built a huge **amphitheater** called the Colosseum. The Colosseum could fit 50,000 people. Some of it is still standing today!

Thousands of people watched gladiator fights in the Colosseum. Sometimes, gladiators would fight one another. Other times, they would take on wild animals, such as tigers, lions, giraffes, and rhinos.

Gladiator fights weren't the only things held at the Colosseum. Sometimes, the amphitheater was used for **executions**. Many times this involved forcing people to fight to the death against wild animals death.

Naumachia shows were another strange kind of entertainment. They involved flooding the amphitheater with water. Ships would sail across the water and recreate famous sea battles for the audience.

GORY GLADIATORS

Many gladiators were **enslaved** people or prisoners. Some gladiators who won their battles and put on good shows became famous. This led to a few Roman **citizens** training to be gladiators for the fame, too.

Gladiators used all kinds of weapons in their battles.

Thraxx (thur-AKS) gladiators used curved swords and wore helmets that covered their entire heads. They fought against the murmillo (MUR-mee-loh) gladiators. Murmillo gladiators used short swords and large shields.

Retiarius (reh-tee-AH-ree-uhs) gladiators did not wear much armor. They used nets and fork-like spears to fight secutor (SI-kyoo-tor) gladiators. Secutor gladiators wore round helmets to avoid getting caught in nets.

HEALTH AND SICKNESS

Ancient Romans believed cabbage could **cure** many things. They used it to treat headaches, wounds, and sores.

DO NOT TRY THESE ANCIENT ROMAN TREATMENTS!

When people in ancient Rome had trouble pooping, they mixed together salt, milk, honey, and wolf **bile**. Then, they put it in their belly buttons.

Jaundice is a health problem that turns the skin yellow. The ancient Romans believed ashes from a dog's skull could treat this condition. They mixed the ashes with honey wine and drank it.

Touching an elephant's trunk was another way to treat headaches. The ancient Romans thought it was even better if the elephant sneezed on the sick person!

PRETTY ROMANS

Looking pretty was important for ancient Romans. The color of their hair was all thanks to hair dye. The dye was made from a mix of ashes, walnut shells, and worms.

Sometimes, Romans wore jewelry that had been dipped in the blood of their favorite gladiators. They also used face creams made with sweat from the gladiators.

Many women in ancient Rome used strange things to help their skin. They used goose fat for their wrinkles. Some thought that the oil from sheep's wool made their skin softer.

Some women wanted their eyebrows and eyelashes to stand out. They used the soot from fires to make these parts darker.

SQUEAKY CLEAN

Ancient Romans used public baths to stay clean. But washing up wasn't the only thing they did there. Romans could also exercise and meet friends at public baths.

AQUEDUCT

People in ancient Rome used aqueducts to get water for their baths. Aqueducts were long channels. The water from lakes or springs flowed down these channels.

The caldarium (kal-DAIR-ee-uhm) was a room in the baths that had pools of hot water. Romans sat in the caldarium to get sweaty. Then, they used a metal tool called a strigil to scrape off dirt and dead skin.

After bathing, the Romans went to the frigidarium (fri-juh-DAIR-ee-uhm). This room helped them cool down with cold water.

ROMAN TOILETS

In ancient Rome, they also had public toilets. But instead of cubicles, the toilets back then were open. This let Romans chat with the people next to them.

Ancient Romans cleaned their behinds with a sponge on a stick. Then, they rinsed the sponge with water running along the floor. With that, the sponge was ready for the next person to use. *Yuck!*

Public toilets were connected to underground sewers. These sewers became homes for many creatures. So, there was always a risk of rats or snakes coming out of a toilet!

Another risk was fire. The gas in the sewers could build up and catch fire.

WASHING WITH PEE

Romans liked to keep their clothes fresh and clean. However, they had a baffling way of washing them.

First, the ancient Romans left pots out in the streets for people to pee into. Once these pots were full, they were taken to a place called a fullonica. There, the pots were left to sit until they were ready to be used.

The pots of pee were poured into a big pit with clay and water. Next, dirty clothes were thrown into the smelly mix. Someone called a fuller then climbed into the pit and stamped on the clothes.

After that, the ancient Romans rinsed the clothes with water and hung them up to dry.

BOYS DID WHAT?

Ancient Roman boys went to school if their families could afford it. If not, they stayed at home and worked with their parents.

1	I	11	XI	30	XXX	
2	II	12	XII	40	XL	
3	III	13	XIII	50	L	
4	IV	14	XIV	60	LX	
5	V	15	XV	70	LXX	
6	VI	16	XVI	80	LXXX	
7	VII	17	XVII	90	XC	
8	VIII	18	XVIII	100	C	
9	IX	19	XIX	500	D	
10	X	20	XX	1000	M	

Boys who went to school were taught how to read and write. In ancient Rome, numbers were written as letters in different combinations. Different groups of letters **represented** different numbers.

Children at Roman schools used wax tablets instead of paper for writing. Letters and numerals were **carved** into the wax. Then, fresh wax could be added so the tablet could be used again.

Boys at school were followed by a paedagogus (PYE-duh-goh-guhs). The paedagogus made sure the boys behaved. If not, the boys could be punished.

GIRLS DID WHAT?

Unlike the boys, girls did not go to school. Rich families hired tutors to teach the girls at home. In families that didn't have the money, girls worked with their parents.

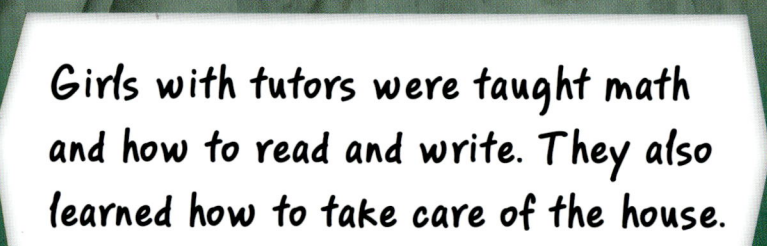

Girls with tutors were taught math and how to read and write. They also learned how to take care of the house.

Large homes in ancient Rome were called villas. Villas were home to families and their servants. Materfamilias were the women in charge of the house.

Materfamilias taught the children. They were often good at math, so they were also in charge of the family's money.

FEASTING TIME

Rich Romans loved to have big feasts to show off to guests. The richer the Roman, the fancier the feast.

Dormice were a fancy treat served to Roman guests. The animals were kept alive in a pot called a glirarium. Inside, the dormice ate and slept all day. This would fatten them up for dinner.

An ancient Roman dining room was called a triclinium. It was decorated with paintings and mosaics. The Romans ate their meals while lying down on sofas.

Roman dinner parties also had entertainment. Performers would often dance or play instruments. Some big feasts even had their own gladiator fights!

BREAKING THE LAW

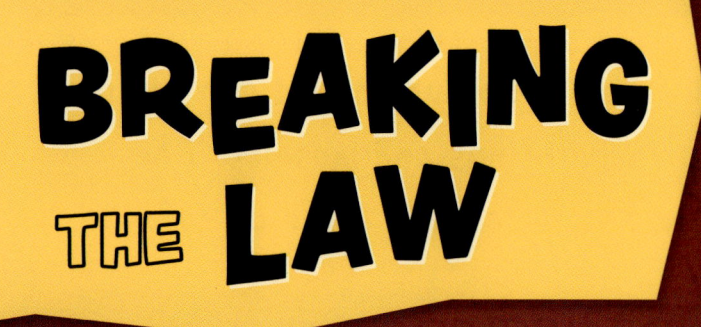

In ancient Rome, citizens had to follow the law. The Twelve Tables were a set of Roman laws that were written on bronze tablets. One law said women could not cry at funerals. Another was about not having meetings at night.

Some citizens avoided getting punished. However, others were not so lucky.

One punishment was to put the **criminal** into a sack with a monkey, a dog, a snake, and a chicken. The sack was tied up and thrown into the sea.

Women at a temple for the goddess Vesta had to make sure a fire stayed burning. If it went out, they were punished by being beaten.

YOUR PLACE IN HISTORY

Do you think you could live in ancient Rome? From washing clothes with pee to sharing sponges to wipe their behinds, the people who lived in the past sure had it rough.

If you think being in ancient Rome was tough, then try reading about another time in period. However, be warned! Wherever you go, you may find yourself thinking . . .

what baffling behavior!

GLOSSARY

amphitheater a building with seats rising in curved rows around an open space

bile a yellowish or dark-green fluid in the liver that helps break down food

carved cut into shape

citizens people who live in a particular country, city, or town

civilization a large group of people that shares the same history or way of life

criminal a person who breaks the law

cure to get rid of an illness completely

enslaved being held captive by other people and forced to work without pay

executions punishments by death

politician a person who is a member of government

represented stood for something else

republic a government where power belongs to the people who make choices by voting

INDEX

READ MORE

Mather, Charis. *The Peculiar Past in Ancient Rome (Strange History).* Minneapolis: Bearport Publishing, 2024.

Troupe, Thomas Kingsley. *Fierce Gladiators (Ancient Warriors).* New York: Crabtree Publishing, 2024.

LEARN MORE ONLINE

1. Go to **FactSurfer.com**
or scan the QR code below.

2. Enter "**Life in Ancient Rome**" into the search box.

3. Click on the cover of this book
to see a list of websites.